SUBTRACT It!

RACHEL FIRST

Consulting Editor, Diane Craig, M.A./Reading Specialist

Sandcastle

An Imprint of Abdo Publishing
abdopublishing.com

abdopublishing.com

Published by Abdo Publishing, a division of ABDO, PO Box 398166, Minneapolis, Minnesota 55439. Copyright © 2016 by Abdo Consulting Group, Inc. International copyrights reserved in all countries. No part of this book may be reproduced in any form without written permission from the publisher. SandCastle™ is a trademark and logo of Abdo Publishing.

Printed in the United States of America, North Mankato, Minnesota

102015
012016

Editor: Liz Salzmann
Content Developer: Nancy Tuminelly
Cover and Interior Design and Production: Mighty Media, Inc.
Photo Credits: Shutterstock

Library of Congress Cataloging-in-Publication Data

First, Rachel, author.
 Subtract it! : fun with subtraction / Rachel First ; consulting editor, Diane Craig, M.A./reading specialist.
    pages cm. -- (Math beginnings)
 ISBN 978-1-62403-935-5
1. Subtraction--Juvenile literature. 2. Arithmetic--Juvenile literature. I. Title.
 QA115.F556 2016
 513.2'12--dc23
                2015020614

SandCastle™ Level: Transitional

SandCastle™ books are created by a team of professional educators, reading specialists, and content developers around five essential components—phonemic awareness, phonics, vocabulary, text comprehension, and fluency—to assist young readers as they develop reading skills and strategies and increase their general knowledge. All books are written, reviewed, and leveled for guided reading, early reading intervention, and Accelerated Reader™ programs for use in shared, guided, and independent reading and writing activities to support a balanced approach to literacy instruction. The SandCastle™ series has four levels that correspond to early literacy development. The levels are provided to help teachers and parents select appropriate books for young readers.

EMERGING · BEGINNING · **TRANSITIONAL** · FLUENT

Contents

SUBTRACTION Action

Subtraction is a kind of math.

$$4 - 2 = 2$$

It tells how many are left.

$$3 - 2 = 1$$

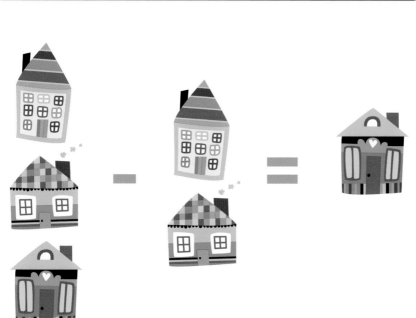

Subtraction is fun and easy.

Start with six leaves.

Take two
leaves away.

Count how many are left.

That's subtraction!

MINUS Sign

9 - 4

minus sign

Subtraction problems use the minus sign. *Minus* means *less*. An **equal** sign goes before the answer.

Here is a number sentence. Read it, "Nine minus four equals five."

equal sign

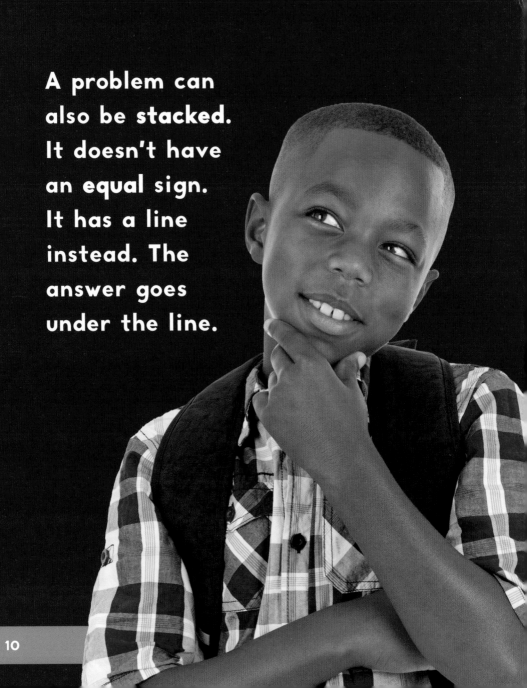

A problem can also be **stacked**. It doesn't have an **equal** sign. It has a line instead. The answer goes under the line.

$$\begin{array}{r} 8 \\ -7 \\ \hline 1 \end{array}$$

$$5-4=$$

$$7-6=$$

$$4-2=$$

$$8-3=$$

$$9-2=$$

Rick likes to subtract.

He has a lot of problems to do.

2-1=

3-1=

9-4=

How many of Rick's problems can you do? Write down the answers.

What's the DIFFERENCE?

The answer to a subtraction problem is called the *difference*.

Grace subtracts
1 from 3. The
difference is 2.

WORD Problems

Math problems can be written with words.

Susan has four apples. She eats one. How many are left?

Eight kids ride the bus. One kid gets off. How many kids are still on the bus?

Number LINES

A number line is just that. It's a line with numbers on it. It can help you do **math**.

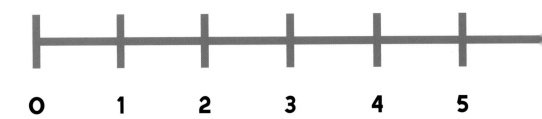

0   1   2   3   4   5

Move to the left to subtract. What is 9 – 3?

Put your finger on the 9. Move three numbers to the left. The answer is 6!

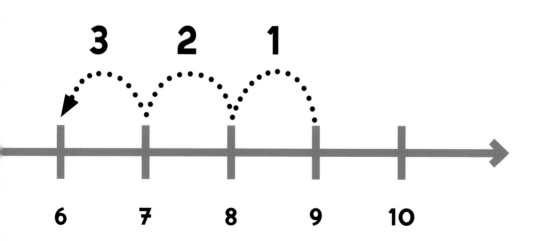

Number lines can help with word problems.

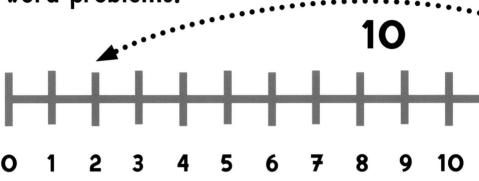

10

0 1 2 3 4 5 6 7 8 9 10

Jess makes twelve cookies.

11 12 13 14 15 16 17 18 19 20

She eats ten cookies. How many are left?

Use the number line to find out!

PRACTICE

Gather ten small things. You should be able to hold them all in your hands. Try buttons, game pieces, or candies.

Draw a large circle on a piece of paper. Drop all ten things on the paper. Count how many landed in the circle. How many are outside the circle? Use subtraction to find out!

10 - 4 = 6

Glossary

EQUAL – having exactly the same size or amount.

MATH – short for mathematics. The study of numbers and shapes and how they work together.

STACK – to put things on top of each other.